EYEWITNESS
Activity

BIRD WATCHER

by David Burnie

REVISED EDITION
Editor Virien Chopra
Assistant Art Editor Nidhi Rastogi
Senior Editors Carron Brown, Bharti Bedi
Senior Art Editors Sheila Collins, Nishesh Batnagar
DTP Designer Pawan Kumar
Senior DTP Designer Harish Aggarwal
Jacket Designers Laura Brim, Dhirendra Singh
Jackets Assistant Claire Gell
Managing Jackets Editor Saloni Singh
Jacket Design Development Manager Sophia MTT
Pre-production Manager Balwant Singh
Producer, Pre-production Gillian Reid
Senior Producer Rita Sinha
Managing Editors Linda Esposito, Kingshuk Ghoshal
Managing Art Editors Philip Letsu, Govind Mittal
Publisher Andrew Macintyre
Associate Publishing Director Liz Wheeler
Design Director Stuart Jackman
Publishing Director Jonathan Metcalf

ORIGINAL EDITION
Produced for Dorling Kindersley Ltd by
Cooling Brown Ltd:
Creative Director Arthur Brown
Editor Kesta Desmond
Designers Tish Jones, Elaine Hewson

For Dorling Kindersley Ltd:
Senior Editor Shaila Brown
Senior Art Editor Stefan Podhorodecki
Managing Editor Linda Esposito
Managing Art Editor Diane Thistlethwaite
Publishing Managers
Caroline Buckingham, Andrew Macintyre
Photography Dave King
Consultant Kim Bryan

First published in Great Britain in 2006
This edition first published in Great Britain in 2015 by
Dorling Kindersley Limited, 80 Strand, London, WC2R ORL

Copyright © 2006, © 2015 Dorling Kindersley Limited
A Penguin Random House Company
2 4 6 8 10 9 7 5 3 1
001–274462–Sep/2015

A CIP catalogue record for this book is available from
the British Library.

ISBN 978-0-2411-8542-1

Colour reproduction by Alta Image Ltd, London, UK
Printed in China

A WORLD OF IDEAS:
SEE ALL THERE IS TO KNOW
www.dk.com

Contents

4   The world of birds
6   Essential equipment
8   Hide and peep
10 Bird buffet
12 Birdfeeders
14 Making a bird table
16 Bird gardening
18 Feeding signs
20 Bird pellets
22 Tracks and trails
24 All about feathers
26 Feathers and flight
28 Birds in the air
30 Bath time
32 Who's who?
34 Courtship
36 Calls and songs
38 Nesting time

40 Making a nestbox
42 Nesting together
44 Starting life
46 Growing up
48 Ducking and diving
50 Birds on the shore
52 Birds about town
54 Nightwatch
56 Brainy birds
58 Flock watching
60 Migration
62 Bird calendar
64 Bird lifespans
66 Helping birds
68 Bird classification
70 Glossary
72 Index

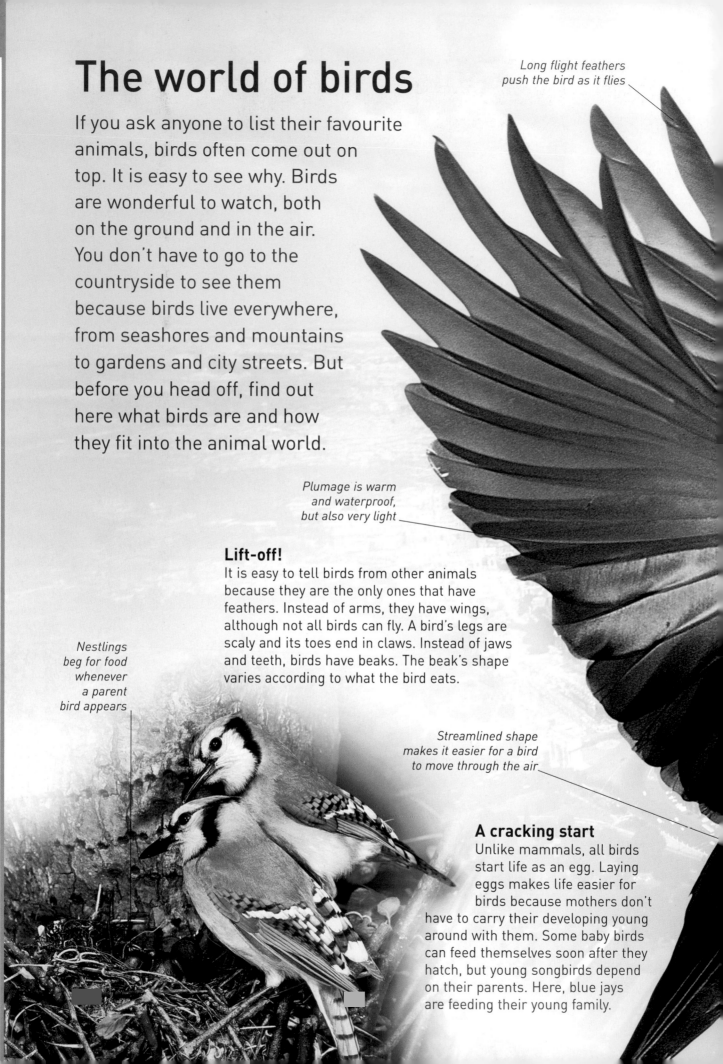

The world of birds

If you ask anyone to list their favourite animals, birds often come out on top. It is easy to see why. Birds are wonderful to watch, both on the ground and in the air. You don't have to go to the countryside to see them because birds live everywhere, from seashores and mountains to gardens and city streets. But before you head off, find out here what birds are and how they fit into the animal world.

Long flight feathers push the bird as it flies

Plumage is warm and waterproof, but also very light

Lift-off!
It is easy to tell birds from other animals because they are the only ones that have feathers. Instead of arms, they have wings, although not all birds can fly. A bird's legs are scaly and its toes end in claws. Instead of jaws and teeth, birds have beaks. The beak's shape varies according to what the bird eats.

Nestlings beg for food whenever a parent bird appears

Streamlined shape makes it easier for a bird to move through the air

A cracking start
Unlike mammals, all birds start life as an egg. Laying eggs makes life easier for birds because mothers don't have to carry their developing young around with them. Some baby birds can feed themselves soon after they hatch, but young songbirds depend on their parents. Here, blue jays are feeding their young family.

ORNITHOLOGY

People who study birds are known as ornithologists. Professional ornithologists work all over the world, studying the way birds live and their habitats. Many are involved in bird conservation. Amateur ornithologists enjoy watching birds and seeing how many types they can spot. Some champion birders have seen more than 9,000 different kinds of birds.

◀ **Getting a good look**
Birdwatchers use telescopes and binoculars to study birds without frightening them away.

Superb eyesight for finding food

Beak designed for catching and holding food

Legs stow away close to the body after take-off

Wild and tame

Birds are wary of people. If they are disturbed, they usually fly away. But with patience, wild birds can sometimes be tamed. This is a great way of seeing birds close up and watching how they behave. To get friendly with a robin, try sitting in the same place every day and offering it some food.

Essential equipment

Birdwatching is something you can do almost anywhere, whether you have a few spare minutes or the whole day. But to get the most out of your birding, it helps to have the right equipment with you. Binoculars are really useful, and so is a bird guide and a notebook and pencil. If you're going on a long outing, it's worth packing some collecting equipment in case you find anything you want to bring home.

BIRDWATCHER'S CODE

When you go birdwatching, do not harm any birds or other wildlife. Follow these four golden rules:

- Try not to disturb the birds you are watching.
- Don't get too close.
- Don't approach birds that are on their nests or with their young.
- Leave baby birds alone. Their parents are almost certainly nearby.

WHAT TO PACK

For birdwatching, you must have some binoculars so that you can study birds from a distance. Tweezers, containers, and a magnifying glass are useful for studying and collecting interesting feathers and bones.

Binoculars ▶
Choose binoculars that magnify between eight and ten times. Avoid large, heavy ones.

Tweezers
Use tweezers with pointed tips

Self-sealing plastic bags

Magnifying glass

Useful for bones and pellets

Small plastic box with lid

Use these for feathers

Keep lens clean

IDENTIFYING BIRDS

When you first start birdwatching, don't be disappointed if you can't identify birds straight away. With practice, you will soon learn what to look for so that you can tell different birds apart. Check these key features and consult the field guide flaps.

◄ Herring gull
It is easy to spot gulls, but harder to tell the species apart. The herring gull has a yellow beak with a red spot, and grey wings with black tips.

- Long-legged birds with extra-long beaks: herons and storks.
- Waterbirds with flattened beaks: ducks, geese, and swans.
- Daytime hunters with sharp claws: birds of prey.
- Night-time hunters with sharp claws: owls.
- Coastal birds with sharp beaks and slender wings: gulls and terns.

- Birds with hooked beaks and colourful plumage: parrots.
- Tiny birds that hover in front of flowers: hummingbirds.
- Birds that perch vertically on tree-trunks: woodpeckers.
- Small birds with musical songs and calls: songbirds.

Out in the open
Birdwatching can take you to some exciting places. Coasts are great places, especially in spring, when seabirds come back to land to breed. Hillsides and open country are good places for spotting birds of prey.

Hide and peep

Birds are very good at spotting movement, which is why it's so easy to scare them away. But unlike us, they don't pay much attention to things that keep still. If you watch birds from a portable hide, they will quickly forget that you are inside. Lots of bird reserves have permanent hides that give visitors an ideal view. But you can make your own portable hide with some netting and bamboo. It's easy to put up and dismantle, so you can take it on all your birdwatching trips.

WHAT YOU WILL NEED

- Four strong bamboo canes about 1.5–2 m (5–6½ ft) long
- 3–4 m (10–13 ft) plastic garden netting
- Ball of strong string
- Leafy twigs. Select these when you are ready to use them.

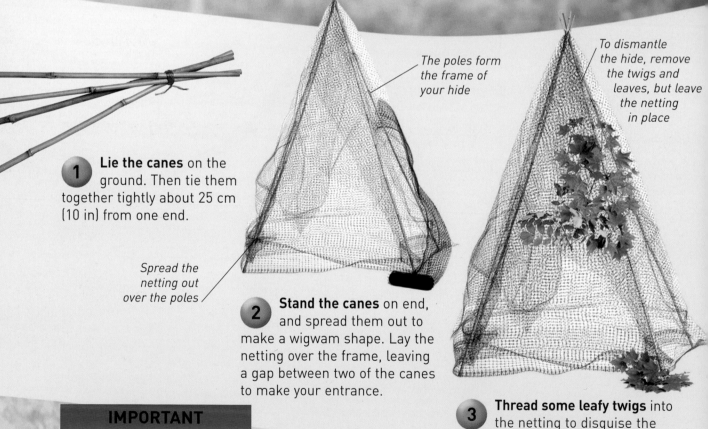

The poles form the frame of your hide

To dismantle the hide, remove the twigs and leaves, but leave the netting in place

1 **Lie the canes** on the ground. Then tie them together tightly about 25 cm (10 in) from one end.

Spread the netting out over the poles

2 **Stand the canes** on end, and spread them out to make a wigwam shape. Lay the netting over the frame, leaving a gap between two of the canes to make your entrance.

3 **Thread some leafy twigs** into the netting to disguise the hide. Leave the entrance clear so that you can get in and out easily.

IMPORTANT

Ssshhh! Birds have very good hearing. Be careful what you pack to eat in your hide. The sound of crackly wrappings will frighten them away.

BIRD EYESIGHT

Your eyes look straight ahead, so you can see only part of what is around you – to see the rest, you have to turn your head. But most birds have eyes that face out to either side. This means that they can see all around them, so they're hard to creep up on. Their eyesight is sharper than ours, too, enabling them to spot tiny insects amongst leaves and grasses.

◀ **All-round view**
A pheasant's eyes look out to each side, and take up nearly half the space in its skull.

4 **Your hide** is now ready for use. It will provide an excellent base for you to observe some of the many species of birds in your area. In the hide, you can use binoculars, and you can also photograph and sketch the birds that you see to help you identify them.

Bird buffet

Some birds will eat almost anything, but most are choosy about their food. Many garden birds enjoy seeds and fruit, but hardly ever touch insects or worms. Others are exactly the opposite. They love anything that runs or wriggles, but they ignore seeds and other food that comes from plants. To find out what food your backyard birds like, try giving them a special buffet. As the birds arrive to feed, you will be able to sort out vegetarians from meat-eaters, and fussy eaters from those that are easy to please.

WHAT YOU WILL NEED

- 6 identical bowls
- Mealworms
- Breadcrumbs
- Sunflower seeds
- Oats, which have been soaked in water
- Animal fat – fatty bacon rind is ideal
- Soft fruit

Make sure the bowls are out of reach of predators like cats.

You can buy mealworms in most angling shops

Seed-eating birds, like this house finch, often eat cereals and sometimes like animal fat as well

Mealworms

Breadcrumbs

Sunflower seeds

Soaked oats

1 **Find an open** area in your back garden, away from bushes and overhanging trees.

2 **Arrange the dishes** in a row, and put a different food in each one. When birds start to arrive, watch them feeding from indoors, or from an outside hideaway.

IMPORTANT

Remember to clear away the buffet before dark – if you don't, it could attract unwelcome visitors such as mice or rats.

FEEDING LEVELS

As well as eating different foods, birds feed at different levels. Thrushes and starlings forage on the ground, but many other birds are used to finding their food in bushes and trees. These birds will visit your bird buffet, but they will not stay long before fluttering back to a perch. Some birds – particularly swifts and swallows – will never come to your buffet, no matter what food you put out. They feed only on flying insects.

Flying food ▲
Swallows get all the food they need by catching insects in the air. During the breeding season, the adults collect insects in their throats so they can take them back to their nests.

HANDY TIP

Include a seed cake, and you can watch the birds feeding, as they can't fly away with it.

Soft fruit

Bacon fat

Bird beaks

By looking at the shape of a bird's beak, you can often work out what kind of food it eats. Some beaks work like tweezers, while others are more like pliers or drinking straws. As well as using their beaks for eating, birds use them for preening, and for collecting materials to make their nests.

Insect eater ▲
Wrens have thin beaks for picking insects and other small animals out of narrow crevices.

Nectar eater ▶
A hummingbird's beak works like a drinking straw, sucking up sugar nectar from flowers.

Meat eater ▲
Owls use their hooked beaks to hold on to small animals, after they have caught them with their claws.

Seed eater ▶
A goldfinch's beak has a sharp point and strong edges for cracking open seeds.

Birdfeeders

Making a feeder is a perfect way to watch birds that feed off the ground. In a few minutes, you can turn a bush or a tree into a feeding station that will be busy all year round. You can hang up some kinds of food with nothing more than a piece of string. Seeds need a special dispenser, so birds can perch as they feed. Seed dispensers are easy to make. If you can find an empty plastic water bottle, try making the one shown here.

A clear bottle is best so the birds can see the seeds inside

Make the feeding holes close to each perch

The bigger the bottle, the longer the seed will last

1 **Push a pencil** or skewer across the bottom of the bottle, so it goes through one side and out the other side. Always push away from your body.

2 **Do the same** thing with a second pencil or skewer, at right angles to the first. You should now have four perches sticking out of the bottle.

3 **Make four holes** with a sharp pencil near the bottom of the bottle – close to each perch – large enough for the seeds to come out.

4 **Fill the bottle** with birdseed, using the funnel. (If you don't have one make a paper cone.) Screw on the cap.

5 **Hang the bottle** from a low branch, by tying one end of the string around the neck of the bottle and the other around the branch.

Half a coconut

WHAT YOU WILL NEED

- Plastic bottle with screw cap
- Pencils or wooden skewers – about twice the width of the bottle
- Plastic or paper funnel
- String
- Birdseed from a pet shop

⚠️ Get an adult to help you make the holes in the bottle.

Hanging out food

You can hang up many kinds of food without needing to make a feeder. Lots of birds like coconut, because it is rich in nutritious oils. Peanuts are also good – either in a string bag, or in their shells. Be careful to use unsalted peanuts, as salted ones can make birds ill.

Peanuts in their shells   Peanuts in string bag

PERFECT PACKAGING

Flower feeder ▲
Some birds feed on the sugary nectar inside flowers. These include hummingbirds in North America, sunbirds in Africa and Asia, and honeyeaters and parrots in Australia. Hummingbirds are easy to attract – all you need is a feeder stocked with sugary water.

Small birds, such as this blue tit, are attracted to hanging dispensers

WHAT YOU WILL NEED

- Weatherproof plywood to following sizes: 30 x 40 cm x 1.5 cm (12½ x 15½ x 1/16 in) for tray; 1.5 m x 1 cm sq (5 ft x ½ in sq), cut into 4 strips, 2 of 40 cm (15½ in), and 2 of 26 cm (10 in) for tray rim; 50 cm x 4 cm sq (19 x 1½ in sq) for postholder; 1.5 m x 4 cm sq (5 ft x 1½ in sq) for post
- 20 mm (1 in) nails
- 55 mm (2 in) screws
- Tape measure • Pencil
- Saw • Hammer
- Electric drill

You will need an adult to help you with the sharp tools.

Making a bird table

If you want to attract birds and watch them feed, a bird table is hard to beat. You can buy bird tables ready-made, but with an adult to help you, it's good fun to make one yourself. The bird table shown here is simple to make, and easy for birds to use. The table sits on a square post, which needs to be hammered into the ground. It has a rim to stop food falling off, and small gaps to let rainwater drain away.

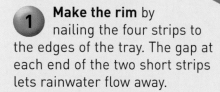

1 **Make the rim** by nailing the four strips to the edges of the tray. The gap at each end of the two short strips lets rainwater flow away.

2 **Cut the timber** for the postholder into four pieces. Drill pilot holes through them, and screw them to the base of the tray. This makes a square holder for the post.

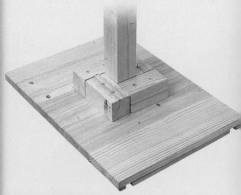

3 **Saw one end** of the post to create a sharp point. Push the other end into the postholder, making sure that it fits tightly.

FEEDING IN WINTER

If winters are cold where you live, feeding birds helps them to get through a difficult time of year. Birds need food to keep warm – if they don't eat enough, they can die of cold during the night. Don't forget to put out water as well as food, because birds can get dehydrated when ponds and puddles are frozen over.

Robin in the snow ▲
Snow makes it harder for birds to find food on the ground.

FEEDING TIME

Once your bird table is ready, don't be tempted to put out too much food. Instead, put out small amounts of different foods, and brush the table clean at least once each week. Instead of putting out large pieces of food, it's best to use ones that are chopped up, or finely divided. This will stop large birds from snatching the food and flying off with it.

Jacket potato

Bread, cake, and biscuit

Pasta, pastry, and rice

Bacon rind

Stale cheese

Fat

Tinned catfood

Fruit

Bird table food ▲

Bread, biscuits, and cereals are all good for your bird table, and so are fruit, cheese, and fat. You can also try petfood – but only in very small amounts.

Birds feel safe on a bird table, because they have an all-round view while they feed

Screw in here to fix post

IMPORTANT

Birds can carry germs. Always wash your hands after you have put out food, or after cleaning away leftovers.

4 **Drill one** or two pilot holes sideways through the postholder, and insert screws to fix the post firmly in place.

5 **To put up** the table, choose a suitable spot and hammer the centre of the tray, driving the post into the ground.

Bird gardening

One of the best ways to help birds is to grow the things they eat. If you do this, birds won't only visit your garden to feed – some of them may decide to use it for nesting, too. Sunflowers are ideal plants to start with. Instead of cutting them down when they are dead, leave them standing so birds can feed on their seeds. As well as sunflowers, birds also love seeds from thistles and other weeds, so try leaving a corner of your garden to go wild.

WHAT YOU WILL NEED

- Sunflower seeds
- Small flowerpots
- Potting compost
- Trowel

3 **After the plants** have flowered, leave them standing so the seeds ripen. In autumn and winter, watch out for finches and other seed-eating birds perching on them to feed.

1 **In the spring,** plant your sunflower seeds. If the soil is warm, plant them directly in the ground using the trowel to make a hole about 5 cm (2 in) deep. If it's cold, plant the seeds in the pots using the potting compost.

2 **When the seeds** start to grow – after about two weeks – thin them out so the plants are at least 50 cm (20 in) apart. If you started them off in pots, transplant them to the garden now.

Each sunflower produces hundreds of seeds

HANDY TIP

See which plants birds visit in the wild, and try growing them yourself.

American goldfinch feeding on a sunflower

Favourite trees

Trees are very important to birds. They provide somewhere to nest and roost, as well as berries and other food. If you want to attract birds to your garden, choose the types of trees that grow wild near your home. Your local birds will know exactly how to use them.

Blue jay ▲
Jays like acorns, which they bury for winter food. But oak trees grow slowly, so if you plant one, don't expect quick results.

Blackbird ▲
In autumn, blackbirds fatten up on berries. Elders and rowans are two of their favourite kinds.

Lorikeet ▶
These parrots feed on nectar and pollen from flowers. In Australia, eucalyptus (gum) trees attract flocks of lorikeets when they are in bloom.

REALLY WILD

Tidy gardeners don't like weeds, but birds really love them. Weeds harbour lots of bugs that birds eat, and they produce nutritious seeds. If you want to encourage birds into your garden, you could try planting a mixture of wildflower seeds. If you want your garden to be really bird-friendly, let a corner get tangled and overgrown, so birds can make their nests inside it.

Seed bank ▶
Thistles hold onto their seeds for many weeks, so birds keep coming back to them for a meal. This European goldfinch is just about to try its luck.

Feeding signs

When birds feed in the wild, they often leave tell-tale signs behind them. Many birds peck at seeds or fruit, but some specialize in the trickier task of opening nuts or cones. A few are expert at smashing open snails, or digging out grubs that bore their way through wood. With a bit of detective work, you can find out where these birds have been feeding. If you're lucky, you may also spot the private larders that some birds make – they use these when fresh food is hard to find.

Scattered scales
This crossbill is extracting seeds from a cone. Its beak works like a pair of cutters, levering the seeds out of the cone and dropping the scales on the ground. Crossbills often feed in flocks, so you may find lots of scales in one feeding place.

WHERE TO LOOK

- Pecked nuts, cones – woods, hedges, parks
- Shrike larders – thorny hedges, barbed wire
- Broken shells – flat rocks near the shore, rocky places inland
- Woodpecker holes – woods, parks, gardens

Skewered snacks
If you are out in the countryside, keep an eye open for insects or small lizards spiked on barbed wire or on thorns. These gruesome remains show that a shrike is in the area. Shrikes skewer their prey to make it easier to eat, and to keep it for later.

Smash and grab
Many birds feed on hard-bodied animals, such as crabs, mussels, and snails. To get at their food, they often have to break it open first. Some drop it from the air, but this thrush is smashing snails against a hard stone.

Stone "anvil" for crushing snail shells

Beak chisels a hole and spear-like tongue stabs prey

Storing food

Instead of eating their food straight away, some birds store it for later. This jay has collected an acorn, and is about to bury it in the ground. Jays bury hundreds of acorns during autumn. Later, in the winter, they dig them up for food.

Breaking and entering

Woodpeckers chisel holes in trees to get at wood-boring grubs. To see where they have been at work, look out for rotten wood that is covered with peck marks, and check the ground for fresh wood chippings. Large woodpeckers also break their way into other birds' nest holes, so they can eat their eggs or chicks.

BEAK CLEANING

When a bird has finished eating, it often flies off to a perch to clean its beak. Unlike mammals, birds cannot lick themselves clean – instead, they wipe their beaks on a twig or a branch. A bird's beak has a base of bone, but the main part is made of the same substance that is in hooves and nails. Just like a fingernail, the outer part grows all the time, so a bird's beak never gets worn down.

A quick wipe ▶
This crow is cleaning its beak after a meal. It perches on a branch and then wipes each side of its beak. When birds do this, you can sometimes hear a hollow sound as the beak hits the wood.

Bird pellets

Unlike us, birds don't have teeth so they can't chew their food. Instead, many of them swallow it whole. Once they have eaten, they often cough up pellets containing feathers, bones, and other hard parts of their food. Unlike droppings, pellets are usually dry. They are quite safe to handle and fascinating to investigate. If you tease them apart, you can see exactly what a bird has been eating.

WHAT YOU WILL NEED

- Some bird pellets
- Plastic tweezers
- Large jar with a screw top lid
- Kitchen sieve
- Washing-up detergent

IMPORTANT

If looking for owl pellets in old buildings, ask an adult to go with you. After examining the bird pellets, put them outside and wash your hands.

1 **Take one** or two pellets and drop them in a jar. Fill the jar with water, and add a single drop of detergent. Put on the cap, and give it a good shake.

2 **Leave to stand** for 10 minutes and then shake again. Open up the cap, and pour the water through the sieve.

3 **Sort through** the remains, using the tweezers. If you look closely, you may be able to tell exactly what the bird has been eating.

PERCHING POSTS

Many predatory birds, such as owls and kingfishers, have favourite perches. They fly back to their perch to eat the food they've caught. Perching posts include fence posts and dead trees, and are great places to find pellets.

◄ **Making a splash**
Kingfishers often perch on low branches by water. Look for white droppings on wood.

WHERE TO FIND PELLETS

All kinds of birds cough up pellets after they feed. The pellets look different, and you'll also find them in different places. The best places to find owl pellets are in old barns and ruined buildings. Wader pellets are easy to spot on muddy shores, while gull pellets are common on flat and rocky coasts. Crow pellets crop up almost anywhere.

Birds and their pellets ▶
An owl, a crow, and a wader are shown with their pellets (not to scale). Crow pellets often contain shiny black spots – these are the wing cases of beetles.

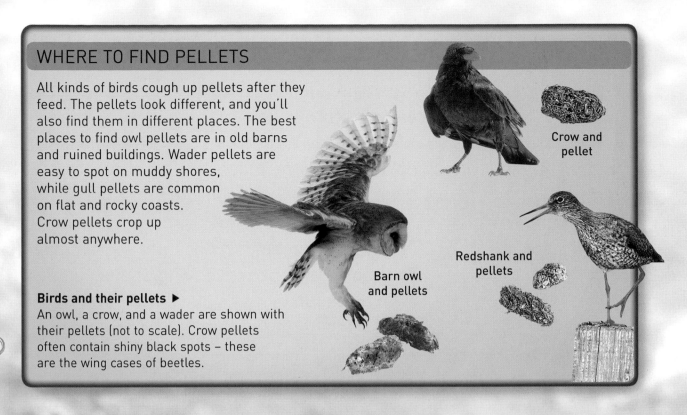

Crow and pellet

Redshank and pellets

Barn owl and pellets

The magnified skull of a vole, found in an owl pellet

WHAT YOU WILL NEED

- Strip of thin card about 25 cm (10 in) sq
- Jug
- Mixing bowl
- Paperclips
- Plaster of Paris
- Scissors
- Spoon
- Water
- Watercolour brush

Tracks and trails

When birds feed in muddy places, they often leave footprints behind them. If you know how to read these tracks, you can tell which birds have been on the move. You'll be able to separate birds that hop from ones that walk, and much more besides. Bird tracks do not last long, because they soon get washed away. You can record them by taking photos, but it's even more fun to make plaster of Paris casts.

1 **Find a clear footprint** in mud that is moist but firm. (Try testing it with your thumb – the hollow it makes should not fill in.) Using the brush, gently clean away any debris or leaves.

2 **Shape the card** into a ring and use the paperclips to fasten it. Place the ring around the print. Press it into the mud, making sure that there are no gaps around the sides.

3 **Mix up some plaster** with the water until it is slightly runny, then pour it into the ring. Leave it for about 15 minutes until the plaster sets.

HOPPERS AND WALKERS

Small birds usually move by hopping, while larger birds walk or run. If you look carefully, you can easily see this difference in their tracks. When birds hop, they leave footprints in pairs, but when they walk, you will see single prints in a line. Because hopping birds are light, their tracks are sometimes difficult to see. Walking birds are heavier, so they leave clearer footprints.

Stealthy mover ▶
Herons often leave very clear tracks, because they stride slowly across soft mud.

These ducks are making prints in the mud as they walk about

Footprint detective

Bird prints can tell you a lot about the birds that made them. Most birds have four toes, but some walk on three. Their toes can be separate, but waterbirds' toes are often joined together by webbing. Look out for these common types of prints.

Songbird ▶
Sparrows, larks, and other songbirds have four slender toes, with one pointing to the rear. They often hop, leaving pairs of prints.

◀ Pigeon
These prints are bigger than a songbird's, with much thicker toes.

Duck or gull ▲
A duck's front toes are joined by webbing, and its hind toe is very short. The prints are at a slight angle, because a duck's feet turn in when it walks.

Moorhen ▲
Moorhens have very long toes, without any webbing. Coot prints are similar, but the toes look fatter, because they have a row of flaps along their sides.

4 **Lift up the plaster,** complete with the card. Leave for 24 hours, and then take off the card. Wash away any mud to leave the print clean.

The plaster will show a raised impression of the print

All about feathers

We don't have feathers, so it's hard for us to imagine how useful they are. Birds use them to fly and to stay warm and dry. Feathers are also great for swimming, and they are ideal for showing off – particularly during the breeding season, when male birds need to attract mates. Birds take good care of their feathers because they have to be in tip-top condition all the year round.

Sink or swim
After a fishing expedition, this cormorant is holding its wings out to dry. A cormorant's plumage is not fully waterproof, so it floats with its body half-submerged. Other waterbirds float like boats because their plumage contains lots of waterproofing oil.

STAYING DRY

Even when it's raining, most birds stay dry because their outer feathers are covered with waterproof oil. If you find a wing feather, you can test this. Hold the feather level, and drip some water on it. The water will roll straight off, leaving the feather perfectly dry.

One bird preens the other's neck – reaching a place the bird can't preen on its own

Preening

Feathers get a lot of wear and tear, so birds preen them to keep them in good condition. To preen itself, a bird uses its beak like a comb, smoothing out its feathers and removing any pieces that have broken off. When it has finished, the bird gives itself a good shake so that its feathers fluff out and then settle back into place.

Wing feathers spread out to dry more quickly

HOW PREENING WORKS

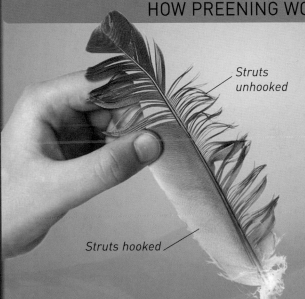

Struts unhooked

Struts hooked

The flat part of a feather is made of short struts linked by tiny hooks. These hooks hold the struts together, giving the feather a smooth surface. But if a bird is busy and active, the hooks often come apart. When this happens, the bird has to preen them back into place. If you find a flight feather, you can try preening it yourself.

◀ **Back into shape**
To "unhook" the feather, pull it through your fingers from the tip to the base. To preen it, gently smooth the struts back into place.

Feathers and flight

Birds often have thousands of feathers, but their flight feathers, which are on a bird's wings and tail, are the most important of all. These feathers are strong but light, and they lift a bird and let it steer as it speeds through the air. Feathers are interesting to study and fun to collect. Flight feathers are easy to find because most birds shed or moult them at least once a year. They replace the old feathers with new ones to make up for wear and tear.

MAKING A FEATHER COLLECTION

Good places to find feathers are under trees, along the sides of lakes and reservoirs, and on the shore. Remember to wash your hands after handling feathers. One of the best ways to store your feathers is to slide them into pieces of corrugated cardboard. You can then paste them in a scrapbook, or put them in a box.

◄ **Safely stored**
Keep your feathers in the dark. Daylight will make them slowly lose their colour.

Macaw flight feather

Feather types

Most birds have four different types of feathers. Flight feathers grow on the bird's wings and its tail – beside the tail feathers. They keep birds airborne, and help them to steer. Body feathers give them a streamlined shape, so they slip easily through the air. Beneath these, fluffy down feathers keep them warm.

Flight feather ▲
These have strong shafts, or quills. The quill is nearest to the feather's front edge.

Down feather ▶
These have small quills, and are soft and fluffy. They trap air next to a bird's body.

Soft fringes muffle the sound of the owl's wings as it hunts

Silent flight

If you find a flight feather, try working out what kind of bird it came from. Owl flight feathers are easy to identify because they have a fringe along their leading edge. These fringes work like silencers, letting owls catch their prey by surprise.

Moulting

In late summer, watch out for birds that have gaps in their wings. These birds are moulting their flight feathers, and replacing them with a new set. Most birds moult their flight feathers gradually, so that they can still fly.

Magpie tail feather

Pheasant tail feather

◄ Body feathers
These are soft and fluffy at the base, but smooth at the tip, giving the bird an even outline.

Tail feathers ▲
These sometimes look like wing feathers, but they have a quill running down the middle, instead of to one side.

Birds in the air

Many birds fly thousands of kilometres, and some stay airborne around the clock until they are old enough to breed. Even if a bird is far away, you can often tell what kind it is by its silhouette, or by the way it flaps its wings. Birds of prey soar high into the sky, with their wings held out straight. Other birds speed past in straight lines or graceful curves. Some flap their wings in bursts, making them bob up and down like boats on the sea.

Hovering

This hummingbird is hovering in front of a flower as it feeds. Its wings can beat up to 200 times a second – faster than any other bird. Apart from hummingbirds and kestrels, most birds hover for only a few seconds at a time.

Tail works like a rudder, steering the bird in a spiral so that it gains height

MID-AIR COLLISIONS

Birds are very good at steering as they speed through the air. Normally, they swerve around buildings, but windows can confuse them. If they see daylight through a window, they sometimes think they can fly straight through, and end up crashing into the glass.

Warning sign ▶
To stop birds flying into windows, try drawing an owl's face on a piece of paper, and sticking it on the inside of the glass. Most birds don't like owls, so they will steer well clear.

Soaring

With its wings spread wide, this Harris's hawk is soaring upwards in a thermal – a column of warm, rising air. Soaring is a great way for a big bird to fly, because the air does most of the work, and the bird hardly has to flap its wings.

Flight feathers are spread out like fingers

Soaring birds have long wings with upturned tips

The hawk suddenly closes its wings if it wants to dive after its prey

Flying styles

Pigeons and doves ▲
These birds usually fly level and straight, flapping their wings all the time. Pigeons and doves are fast fliers. They often fly in flocks, particularly during the winter.

Finches ▲
Finches flap their wings in short bursts, which makes them rise and fall through the air. They often take off, and then fly a short distance before landing on the ground.

Swifts ▲
Except when they are breeding, swifts stay high up in the sky. They twist and turn at high speed, flapping their wings for a few seconds, and then gliding.

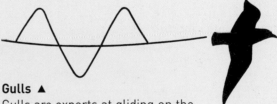

Gulls ▲
Gulls are experts at gliding on the wind. Normally, they move in gentle curves, but they can also hang in the air on the strong sea breeze.

Woodpeckers ▲
It's easy to recognize woodpeckers because they bob up and down as they fly. They flap their wings in bursts, and then close them for a second or more.

Bath time

Birds love taking baths because it keeps their feathers in top condition. They sometimes bathe in dust, but really enjoy a splash in water. Birds don't like a long soak. They prefer a quick dip in shallow water in case they need to make an emergency getaway. If you can find a dustbin lid and a few bricks, you can make the kind of bath that they like. Then you can watch how birds go about washing, and how they preen their feathers afterwards.

WHAT YOU WILL NEED

- Dustbin lid (metal or plastic)
- Some small pebbles
- Three bricks or blocks of wood
- Water

1 **Choose a spot** on open, level grass or bare ground and arrange the bricks in a triangle.

2 **Put the upturned lid** on the bricks and adjust it until it is stable. Spread the pebbles over the deepest part of the bath.

3 **Pour cold water** into the bath until the level is about 2 cm (¾ in) below the rim.

Clean the bath and replace the water regularly

3 **Watch the bath** from indoors or from an outside hideaway. If you have binoculars, train them on the bath so you are ready to watch when the first birds arrive.

DUST BATHS

In dry weather, birds often use dust to keep their feathers clean. They crouch down on the ground and fluff themselves up so that the dust gets deep into their plumage. The dust acts like talcum powder, cleaning the bird's skin and feathers. Game birds such as chickens, grouse, and partridges enjoy taking dust baths, and never take baths in water.

◄ **Dust up**
This partridge is taking a dust bath to clear away parasites and flakes of dead skin from its feathers.

Birds flutter their wings to splash water all over their bodies

IMPORTANT

Make sure that you put the bath in an open place so cats cannot ambush the birds as they wash.

Who's who?

It's easy to tell people apart, but can you do the same with birds? With pet birds, it's not too difficult, but with wild birds it can be hard. To our eyes, one seagull looks very much like another, and the same is often true of garden birds. But birds are individuals, just like people. With a bit of practice, you can sometimes pick a particular bird out from the crowd. The trick is to look at their markings – some birds have unusual features that make them easy to identify – and to notice the way that they behave.

Bird lookalikes

If you watch a flock of gulls, it's easy to tell their age: grown-up gulls have white bodies, but young ones are mottled and brown. Telling adult gulls apart is much harder. They have identical markings, so you need a sharp eye to keep track of individual birds.

ODD BIRD OUT

Look out for albino birds – they have white feathers that really stand out. Partial albinos have a scattering of white patches, or a splash of white on their wings. Full albinos are white all over, making them easy to spot in a crowd. Another oddity to look for is a kink or bump in a bird's beak. Bumps usually develop after the beak has been injured in some way.

Partial albino blackbird ▲
Instead of being black all over, this albino blackbird has white patches on its body, wings, and tail.

FIRST IN THE QUEUE

Behaviour is a good way of telling similar birds apart. Birds aren't polite – instead, some birds push their way to the front to feed, while others get forced to the back. When two birds try to eat the same thing, the dominant bird often makes the weaker one wait, or drives it away. Flocks often have a "pecking order", with older and more experienced birds keeping younger ones under control.

Fighting over food ▲
These two fieldfares look the same, but the dominant bird will get the biggest share of the food.

Familiar faces

Some birds have variable markings – often on the head, or neck and chest – that can help you to tell them apart. In flocking birds, these markings work like badges, helping the members of the flock to know each other. If you study birds in this way, you may recognize individual birds, too.

◄ Cape sparrow 1
Narrow white throat band separated by wide black bar

Cape sparrow 2 ▶
Broad white throat band with thin black bar

◄ Cape sparrow 3
Wide black bar and black chest patch with ragged lower edge

Courtship

The breeding season is the busiest time in any bird's life. For male birds, it starts with the important task of finding and attracting a mate. Many birds do this by singing, or by showing off their fine plumage to catch the female's eye. If the female is interested she comes closer, and often joins in a special dance. During the dance, the two partners get used to each other – a vital step if they are to work together as a team.

They show off their feathery crests as they dance

The grebes mirror each other's actions

Courtship dances

Swimming face to face, these two great crested grebes are halfway through their courtship dance. Lakes and reservoirs are great places to watch birds courting because they are almost always out in the open. Grebes' courtship dances are slow and elegant, but ducks are not nearly so graceful. Male ducks often chase the females, splashing and quacking noisily as they try to push their rivals out of the way.

IMPORTANT

Birds are often shy during the breeding season. If you watch birds courting, try not to disturb them because you may scare away the female.

35

Claiming a territory

This male robin is attacking a stuffed one that has been placed inside his territory. He has mistaken it for a rival male and is trying to chase it away. Territorial skirmishes are common during the breeding season. Territory owners let female birds in because they are potential mates, but chase away males. You won't be able to see the edges of these territories, but male birds know exactly where they are.

WHERE TO LOOK

- Courtship dances – on lakes and reservoirs to see waterbirds, in towns and cities to see pigeons.
- Bird territories – in parks and gardens to see songbirds (watch out for skirmishes when rival males arrive).
- Courtship feeding – on shores and sandbanks to see terns, in gardens to see songbirds.

Courtship feeding

Here, a female tern is being given a fish by her mate. If you see one adult bird being fed by another, it is usually a sign that the two have paired up and are about to breed. The female bird often crouches down with her mouth open and quivers her wings, which is exactly how a baby bird begs for food.

Dressing up

If you watch songbirds or ducks during the breeding season, it is easy to spot the males. Their plumage is often bright and colourful, while females tend to be duller. The male's bright plumage helps him attract a mate. The female's plumage camouflages her while she sits on the nest.

Northern cardinal ▲
With their scarlet plumage, male cardinals are some of the most colourful garden birds in North America. The females are brown with a red tinge.

Redstarts ▲
Male European redstarts have colourful red breasts and black masks on their faces. Females are a rusty colour to disguise them when sitting in nest holes.

Superb fairy wrens ▲
Australian fairy wrens are famous for their beautiful colours. Both sexes have long tails, but only the males are brightly coloured. The females are grey or brown.

Calls and songs

Even when you cannot see birds, you will often hear their calls and songs. Birds use sound to keep in touch, to warn of danger, and to attract mates. Normally, birds keep their distance from noisy humans, but if they hear a bird caller, they will often flutter down to investigate. Bird callers are easy to make. The one shown here produces a fluty sound. Try it out next time you go on a birdwatching walk.

1 **Spread a line** of glue down the centre of the card. Position the marker pen at one end of the card and roll the card up tightly. Secure the end of the card with sticky tape.

ALARM CALLS

Close escape ▲
For city birds, prowling cats are enemy number one.

Many birds sound the alarm when something dangerous gets too close. Compared to songs, alarm calls are usually short and sharp. They do not vary much from bird to bird. If you hear an alarm call, take a closer look. You will often find that a cat is on the prowl. Birds sometimes follow cats from a safe distance, calling noisily. This makes it harder for cats to hunt because it tells all the birds in the area that a predator is on the prowl.

2 **Cut a 5 cm (2 in) slot** along the card. Next, stand the tube on the thicker piece of card and draw around it twice. Cut out the outlines to get two discs.

3 **Glue one disc** on one end of the tube. Make a hole in the middle of the other disc, large enough for the string to go through.

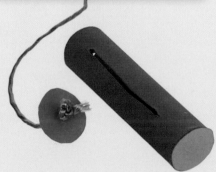

4 **Thread some string** through the hole and tie a knot in the end. Stick the disc to the tube with the knot inside. Your caller is now ready.

WHAT YOU WILL NEED

- Thin card about 8 cm (3 in) x 30 cm (12 in)
- Piece of thicker card
- Large, round marker pen
- Glue
- Sticky tape
- Scissors with sharp tips
- Ballpoint pen
- String

Ask an adult to help when using sharp scissors.

GIFTED MIMICS

Australian impressionist ▲
Lyrebirds can mimic the calls of many animals, including a dog's bark.

Most birds learn their songs by copying adults of their own kind. But some copy other sounds including farm machinery and mobile phones. The world's best mimics include parrots, mynahs, and lyrebirds, as well as some small songbirds.

HANDY TIP

For the best results, make sure that you cut the slot with neat edges.

A narrow slit makes a high-pitched sound, and a wide slit makes a low-pitched sound

5 **To use the caller**, hold the string and whirl the caller around your head. As it rushes through the air, it will make a noise.

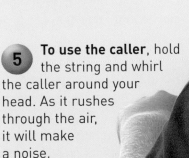

Nesting time

Before birds can raise a family, most of them have to first make a nest. Even if they have never built a nest before, they know exactly what shape to make it, and what building materials to use. You can lend them a hand by putting out some of these materials in your garden. If you stand back and watch the birds arrive, you'll be able to see what they choose.

IMPORTANT

Don't disturb nesting birds. during the breeding season. Watch them from a distance, but never try to get close up to their nests.

Small twigs make a good framework for a nest

Straw is an ideal nesting material

WHAT YOU WILL NEED

- 6 shallow dishes
- Wet mud
- Moss
- Small twigs
- Straw
- String cut into short lengths
- Sheep's wool collected from a farm, or short lengths of knitting wool

1 **Put the materials** into dishes and out in the open where birds can spot them – near the edge of a lawn is ideal. Make sure the mud is soft and moist. Leave the dishes alone for at least 24 hours, so your local birds have time to get used to them.

2 **Watch from** a distance to see which materials they take, and how they carry them. Who does the collecting? The male, the female, or both?

Blue tits and their relatives line their nests with mud

NEXT DOOR NEIGHBOUR

For some birds – including sparrows and starlings – houses make good nesting places. If you check out the buildings in your neighbourhood, you can often spot places where birds have moved in. Nesting materials poking out of holes or beneath roofs, and splashes of white droppings are signs that birds have set up home.

Sparrow ▲
Thriving house sparrows nest on buildings all over the world, and eat the food that people drop.

Small songbirds use moss to insulate their nests

BIRDS WITHOUT NESTS

Instead of building a nest, some birds lay their eggs straight onto the ground. Many seabirds lay their eggs directly on rocky ledges, and terns lay theirs on shingle. Lots of desert and grassland birds are ground-nesters, because their habitats contain very few trees. Ground-nesting birds often have camouflaged eggs and chicks, which makes it harder for predators to find them.

Hollow home ▶
Terns lay their eggs in a hollow, called a scrape, which they dig out with their feet.

Making a nestbox

For birds, good nesting sites can be tricky to find. You can help them by putting up a nestbox in your garden or near your home. Most pet shops sell nestboxes but, with an adult's help, you can make one out of a single piece of wood. The nestbox on these two pages is designed for birds that nest in holes. If you keep the entrance hole small, hole-nesters will be able to get in, but unwelcome, larger visitors will be kept outside.

WHAT YOU WILL NEED

- Piece of weatherproofed plywood 1.5 m (5½ ft) x 15 cm (6 in), 1.9 cm (¾ in) thick
- 3.5-cm (1½-in) galvanized nails
- Two 5-cm (2-in) screws
- Some 1-cm (½-in) tacks
- Piece of rubber inner tube, about 15 cm (6 in) square
- Woodworking tools
- Sandpaper

Ask an adult to help. Woodworking tools can be dangerous.

Side a
250 mm (10 in)
200 mm (8 in)

Side b
200 mm (8 in)
250 mm (10 in)

Front c
200 mm (8 in)

Roof d
212 mm (8½ in)

Base e
112 mm (4½ in)

Back f
450 mm (17¾ in)

150 mm (6 in)

1 **Cut the plywood** into six pieces, as shown on the left. Use sandpaper to smooth down any rough edges.

2 **Using a drill** or a saw, cut the entrance hole. Select one of the sizes below. The hole should be nearer the roof than the base so that cats cannot reach the eggs or nestlings.

Size	Birds
29 mm (1⅛ in)	Tits only
32 mm (1¼ in)	House sparrows, nuthatches
45 mm (1¾ in)	Starlings

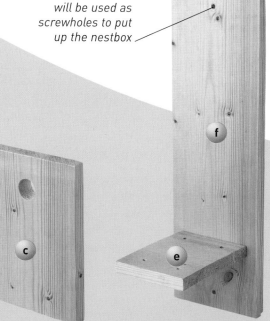

Small holes will be used as screwholes to put up the nestbox

3 **Drill two small holes** in the back, above and below where the box will be. Drill several small holes in the base to let rainwater drain away, then fix the box to the back.

The right site

Birds will use a nestbox only if it is in the right place. For hole-nesting birds, such as tits, tree trunks or walls are ideal. The box must face away from the midday sun so that the nestlings do not get too hot. There should be some leafy cover, but make sure that no branches or twigs are too close to the front door.

Screw the nestbox firmly to a wall or a tree

TREE-HOLE NESTERS

Tree-holes make good homes for birds because they keep nestlings warm and dry. Very few birds, apart from woodpeckers, can make holes for themselves. Instead, they use hollows in rotting wood, or they take over holes that woodpeckers have used and then abandoned. If you are out birdwatching, it is worth giving dead trees a special check. Look out for holes that are partly sealed with mud. Some birds use this technique to keep out intruders.

◄ Homemakers
Woodpeckers make holes that are used by lots of other birds, such as tits, bluebirds, owls, and parrots. Many of them lay their eggs on a bed of feathers and wood chippings.

4 **Assemble the pieces** as shown here, then nail on the piece of rubber to work as a hinge. The box does not need a perch, because this could help predators to get in. Fix the box in position using nails or screws. Ideally, it should be at least 2 m (6½ ft) above the ground.

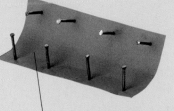

Hinged lid allows cleaning once the nestlings have grown up

Nesting together

Most garden birds like their privacy and nest on their own. But if you go birdwatching in the countryside or on the coast, you will sometimes see birds that nest together in groups. Birds nest together for safety or because good nesting spots are few and far between. Some nesting groups, or colonies, contain 20 or 30 birds, but the largest can contain more than a million. The sight of so many birds can be an unforgettable experience, as can the noise – and sometimes the smell!

Living on a ledge

For humans, cliffs can be very dangerous, but for seabirds they are often a safe place to nest. High up on rocky ledges, these kittiwakes and their chicks are very hard for predators to reach. Kittiwakes make cup-shaped nests from seaweed and mud, but many other seabirds lay their eggs directly on the rock.

WHERE TO LOOK

Coastal cliffs and offshore islands are the best places to see seabird colonies. Visit in spring or early summer. At other times of the year, most of the birds will be out at sea.

Parent spreads its tail to brake

Housemartins make bowl-shaped nests, with a small entrance at the top

IMPORTANT

Take great care when watching cliff-nesting birds. It is easy to lose your balance when you are watching birds in flight. If you are using binoculars, sit down.

Under the eaves

Some colony-forming birds nest close to our own homes. Swallows nest in outbuildings and barns, while housemartins often build their nests underneath eaves. These birds usually choose the same place year after year. They make their nests from wet mud, so they need to have damp ground nearby.

TETCHY NEIGHBOURS

Gannets often nest on rocky islands a long way offshore. Here they are safe from most of their enemies, but they have to be careful of each other. With so many birds crowded together, every pair jealously guards its small patch of rock. If a bird lands in the wrong place, it risks a vicious peck. Young birds must be careful too. Neighbours will attack them if they wander within pecking range.

Touchdown ▶
Gannets recognize their mates by their calls. When a gannet comes in to land, it listens for its partner and then drops down next to their nest.

Starting life

When their nests are ready, female birds get on with the important task of laying eggs. Then the mother sits on her eggs to incubate them. With some birds, the parents take turns at this job, but for most it is a task for the female alone. Inside the eggs, the warmth does its work, and soon the baby birds are big enough to hatch. It's time to keep your distance because nesting birds must not be disturbed.

Incubation

This kestrel has laid a clutch of six eggs and has settled down to incubate them. Every few hours, she rolls the eggs around with her beak to make sure that none of them get cold. While she is sitting on the nest, her mate keeps her supplied with food.

Shell detective

When nestlings hatch, parent birds often pick up the shells and carry them away from the nest. It's a good security system because it makes it less likely that predators will spot the nest. During the nesting season, you will often see pieces of broken shell on the ground. By looking closely, you can sometimes tell what kind of bird laid the egg.

American robin ▶
Like many other birds in the thrush family, the robin lays blue eggs. They make cup-shaped nests lined with mud.

Sparrowhawk ▶
The sparrowhawk lays camouflaged eggs, like most birds of prey. It makes a platform-shaped nest out of sticks.

PERFECT PACKAGING

Eggs have a hard outer shell and a flexible inner lining. The shell gets its strength from calcium, a mineral that birds eat in their food. You can see how calcium works if you leave an egg in vinegar overnight. Some of the calcium will dissolve and the egg will become soft and rubbery.

1 **Half-fill** a jam jar with vinegar and put a chicken's egg inside. Loosely screw on the cap and leave the egg for at least eight hours.

2 **Pour away the vinegar** and try squeezing the egg with your fingers. Instead of cracking, the egg will bend.

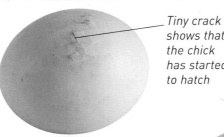

Tiny crack shows that the chick has started to hatch

Chick pushes with its feet to widen the crack

Hatching

When a baby bird hatches, it has to break through its eggshell and into the outside world. Like many birds, this tawny owl chick uses its egg tooth, a hard bump on the tip of its beak. After each peck, the chick turns inside the egg so that it cuts a crack right around the shell. Eventually, one end of the shell breaks away and the chick tumbles out into the nest.

IMPORTANT

It is against the law to take eggs from wild birds' nests. Don't be tempted to go near nests because the parents may abandon their young.

Newly hatched owl chicks are blind and almost featherless

◄ Long-tailed tit
Tits lay up to 12 eggs in a cup-shaped nest. Their shells are white with a pattern of darker speckles or blotches.

◄ Guillemot
Guillemots nest on bare rocky ledges. Their eggs have a sharp point, which helps to stop them rolling off.

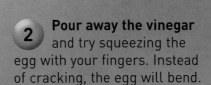

Wood warbler ►
Songbirds often lay speckled eggs. Most songbirds nest in bushes, but the wood warbler nests on the ground.

Growing up

If you have a nestbox in your garden, you will be able to see just how quickly birds grow up. Most people get by on just three meals a day, but baby songbirds need many more. Their parents have to work flat out to keep them fully fed. By watching them for just 15 minutes, you can estimate how many times they bring food to the nest in a day.

WHAT YOU WILL NEED

- Binoculars
- Timer or wristwatch
- Notebook
- Pencil • Calculator
- Calendar or diary

It is essential that you find a nest you can observe without disturbing the birds in any way.

1 Pick a place where you can watch parent birds at work without disturbing them. They should not even know you are there.

2 Set your timer to 15 minutes, or note the time on your watch. You are now ready to start counting.

3 Make a mark in your notebook each time one of the parents arrives at the nest with food. Keep counting until the 15 minutes are up.

4 Use a calendar or diary to work out how many hours there are between sunrise and sunset. The parents are busy from dawn to dusk, so this will give you the length of their working day.

A QUICK START

Birds that nest on the ground grow up even faster than ones that nest in bushes or in trees. You can see this by watching ducklings or goslings in your local park. They can swim and feed when they are just three hours old. They instinctively follow their mother wherever she goes – even if it means crossing busy roads.

◄ **Close family**
Goslings keep close to their mother, but they find their own food.

PARENTS ON GUARD

Some birds go to great lengths to defend their eggs or young. Crows croak noisily if you get too near their nests, and terns and gulls often dive-bomb people to scare them away. If you are in an open, grassy place or on the shore, look out for any bird that seems to be trailing a broken wing. The chances are that it is playing a trick, and trying to distract you from its nest or young.

Follow me! ▶
This killdeer is pretending to be injured so that predators will be distracted and ignore its nest.

5 **Add up** the number of marks in your notebook and multiply the total by four. Finally, multiply this figure by the number of hours in the birds' day. The result is the number of trips the parents make in a day.

Parent blue tit arriving with a caterpillar in its beak

Nestlings' brightly coloured mouths attract their parents

IMPORTANT

If you find a baby bird on its own, don't pick it up unless you are certain that it is injured. Its parents are probably close by, waiting for you to go away.

Ducking and diving

Wherever there is freshwater, there's a good chance that you will find ducks, and perhaps geese and swans. These birds are often used to humans, which makes it easy to watch them feeding. Ducks and their relatives have different ways of finding things to eat. You can observe their feeding techniques by throwing them a mixture of food that floats and food that sinks.

WHAT YOU WILL NEED

- Two glasses of water
- Breadcrumbs
- Rice soaked overnight and drained

HANDY TIP

Make ducks gather round by pretending to scatter some food before you start the test.

1 **To see** how the feeding test will work, put some dry breadcrumbs in a glass of water. Because the food is full of air, it will float near the water's surface.

2 **Soak the rice** overnight, then drain it. Mix it with some more dry breadcrumbs and put a bit of the mixture in a glass of water. The weight of the rice will make the food sink.

3 **Take some** dry breadcrumbs and soaked rice mixture to a local pond or lake and scatter them into the water. Watch how the ducks collect bread from the surface and rice from the bottom.

FEEDING OUT OF WATER

Geese have webbed feet and are very good swimmers. They often spend the night on water but, unlike ducks, they usually feed on land. Geese have strong beaks that are ideal for feeding on plants. Instead of biting off their food, they grip it tightly, and then pull it off with a sharp tug. In winter, geese often feed in large flocks in fields and marshland.

Snow geese ▶
These geese breed in the chilly tundra of northern Canada and spend the winter in warmer places, such as California, USA.

FEEDING STYLES

Some ducks collect food from the surface of the water. Others tip up on end to reach food on the bottom in shallow water. Diving ducks plunge beneath the surface and swim down to get food.

This mallard has up-ended to reach food beneath the surface

Beaks and feeding

Ducks, geese, and swans have the same overall shape, but their beaks and necks are different. This helps them to get at different kinds of food. A few of them feed on fish, but most eat plants or small water animals such as insects, snails, and worms. Their beaks have sensitive tips, so they can feel food they cannot see – a great advantage if the water is muddy.

Dabbling beak ▶
A mallard's beak is long and broad – the ideal shape for collecting food on the water's surface, or for feeling for it in the mud on the bottom.

Mallard

Sifting beak ▶
Shelducks collect food on mudbanks at low tide. They sift through the mud with their beaks, moving their heads from side to side and walking forwards, leaving zigzag tracks in the mud.

Shelduck

Gripping beak ▶
Geese and swans use their beaks to tug at their food. They have strong jaw muscles that can clamp their beak tightly shut.

Black swan

Fishing beak ▶
A merganser's beak is unusually narrow, with serrated edges and a hooked tip. This bird dives to catch fish, and the serrations give it a good grip.

Merganser

Birds on the shore

The shore is a great environment for spotting birds and for seeing how they get their food. Gulls are natural scavengers. They search the shore from the air, swooping on dead remains and anything edible that people leave behind. Other shorebirds, such as oystercatchers and turnstones, search the shore on foot. They like molluscs, shrimps, and worms, and they each have their own ways of dealing with their food. The best time to watch shorebirds is at low tide, when they are busy looking for a meal.

WHERE TO LOOK

- Oystercatchers – on rocky and muddy shores, sometimes in damp fields a little way inland.
- Turnstones – on sandy and muddy beaches.
- Avocets – in shallow bays with muddy bottoms.
- Gulls – on shores of all kinds, also in city parks.
- Terns – on sandy and rocky shores, also near lakes inland.

Oystercatchers use their beaks to open shells and to probe for worms

IMPORTANT

If you go birdwatching along the shore, remember to check the time of high tide, or you could get cut off when the tide comes in.

Cracking open a meal

With their pencil-sized beaks, oystercatchers have just the right equipment for eating animals that live inside shells. To open small shells, an oystercatcher often uses its beak like a hammer, smashing open a hole. With larger shells, it uses it like a screwdriver, prising the two halves of the shell apart. Oystercatchers are noisy birds – listen out for their loud "kleep-kleep" calls.

Tideline food

When the tide drops, a line of seaweed is often left on the shore. Some birds, like the turnstone, flip over the seaweed to find animals underneath. If you try it for yourself, you will see tiny sandhoppers scatter across the beach. Gulls also search the tideline, looking for the remains of fish and crabs.

The turnstone uses its short beak to flip over seaweed, or to prise open shells

Its plumage becomes more colourful in summer, when it migrates to the far north to breed

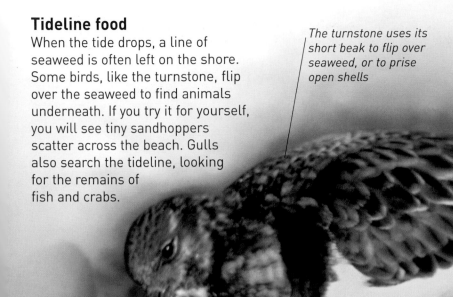

FEELING FOR A MEAL

On low-lying shores, lots of small animals hide away in mud or move about in muddy water. Birds cannot see these tasty treats, but they can find them by using their beaks. Most wading birds have beaks with sensitive tips. They probe the mud or sweep their beaks through the water, feeling for anything that might be food. The moment they touch something tasty, their beaks snap shut and they pull their catch to the surface.

Sweeping up ▶
These American avocets use their up-curved beaks to catch animals in muddy water. They wade through the water, sweeping their beaks from side to side.

Birds about town

You don't have to be in the countryside to go birdwatching, because some birds are perfectly at home in cities and towns. Compared to country birds, they are often quite tame. Their favourite haunts include gardens and parks, but some live right in the middle of town among buildings and on busy streets. Try making a habitat map of your nearest town. Once you have done that, you can visit each habitat to find out which birds use it as their home.

WHAT YOU WILL NEED

- Large piece of white paper
- Coloured pencils
- Small pieces of white card for notes
- Noticeboard and pins
- Selection of bird pictures from magazines

1 **Draw a map** of your local area, showing various different habitats, such as houses, gardens, woodlands, and ponds. Pin the map to the noticeboard. Visit each habitat and make notes of any birds you see and what they are doing.

2 **Make a card** for each habitat. Write some information about the birds you saw at the top of each card. Then look in magazines for pictures of the birds you saw. Cut them out and stick them to the cards. Pin the cards in the correct places on your habitat map.

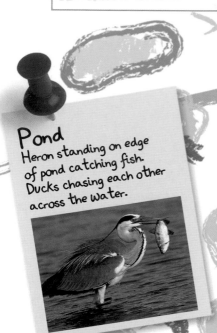

Pond
Heron standing on edge of pond catching fish. Ducks chasing each other across the water.

CITY SCAVENGERS

Cities are great places for birds that eat what we throw away. Gulls and crows are some of the most successful urban scavengers. They are inquisitive and aggressive, and this helps them to get meals. Pigeons and starlings are not quite so pushy, but they are experts at spotting food the moment it hits the ground.

◀ **Easy pickings**
Scavenging birds often gather at rubbish dumps. Here, scavenging gulls are being frightened off by a bulldozer, but they will soon return.

Marsh
Lapwings in a flock on marshy ground near river. Warblers calling among the reeds.

River
Kingfisher diving into water then sitting on perch to eat fish.

Houses
House sparrows nesting in a wall. Often come to the bird table to feed.

Woods
Spotted woodpecker climbing up trees. Stays behind tree to keep out of sight.

Grass
Flock of starlings feeding in grassy field. Crows sometimes chase the starlings away.

River

 Pond

 Marsh

 Grass

 Woods

 House and garden

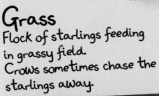

Nightwatch

The owl uses its wings and tail as brakes when it nears the ground

When the sun sets, most birds roost, or go to sleep. But some do exactly the opposite. For owls and nightjars, dusk is the start of the day. To see these birds, or to hear them, you need to be in the right place at the right time. The best time to start your nightwatch is just before sunset. This will give your eyes plenty of time to get adjusted as the light fades away.

IMPORTANT

If you plan to go birdwatching after sunset, make sure that you take an adult with you. Pick somewhere in the open, well away from roads.

Feeding in the dark

This owl is swooping down on its prey with its claws outstretched. Owls catch most of their food on the ground, but they also snatch small birds that are roosting on the branches of trees. Some owls even feed on frogs and fish.

Noises in the night

If you listen quietly after sunset, you may hear birds calling. Owls hoot and screech, while nightjars make purring or buzzing sounds as they fly through the air. In summer, these birds are sometimes joined by songsters like this nightingale, which stays awake all night long.

When birds sleep, their toes lock on to their perch

A safe night's sleep

These pigeons are settling down to roost on a branch. By sticking together, they get a safer night's sleep. Most garden birds roost on their own, but many other kinds stick together. If you watch the evening sky, particularly near reservoirs, lakes, and parks, you will often see birds flying in before night falls.

Flying tonight

It is difficult to spot birds with a torch because they are often on the move. Instead, a better way to spot them is to find a place with a clear view of the setting sun. Just after sunset, you will see birds, and often bats, silhouetted against the sky. To tell which is which, look carefully at their shapes, the way they fly, and their path through the air. Binoculars work well just after sunset because they gather up light and make things easier to see.

Owl ▲
Barn owls fly slowly, with a dipping motion and steadily flapping wings. They criss-cross fields and verges, listening for sounds from small animals on the ground. Other owls fly more quickly, and stop more often to settle on perches.

Nightjar ▲
Nightjars start to feed at dusk. They fly close to the ground in wide circles, scooping up insects in their beaks. Males sometimes touch their wingtips together to make a sharp slapping sound. This is a call sign to females.

Bat ▲
Bats chase individual insects, and their flightpath is full of sudden twists and turns. Their wings flap much more quickly than a bird's. Bats often hunt over water, sometimes dipping down to drink.

Brainy birds

Birds do not have a great reputation for being brainy, but they can be smart when they are trying to get at food. You can see this for yourself by offering them a tasty snack. The snack is in two pots. One pot is open, so the food is easy for birds to reach, but the other has a lid. Humans know that lids have to be opened, but can your garden birds work this out?

WHAT YOU WILL NEED

- Two small, transparent, flat-based plastic pots
- Bird seed
- A small piece of stiff cardboard or paper
- Sticky tape or masking tape
- Small pebbles
- Scissors
- Pen or pencil

Bird seed mix

1 **Put one pot** upside down on the piece of card and draw a circle around it. Put the card to one side. Next, half-fill both pots with pebbles – these will stop birds knocking over the pots when they feed.

2 **Make a lid** for one of the pots by cutting around the circle on the card. Leave a small tab sticking out. Fasten the lid in place by making a hinge with sticky tape.

3 **Put a small quantity** of seeds in both pots and close the lid. Put the pots outside, close together.

BIRDS WITH AMAZING MEMORIES

In late summer and autumn, watch out for jays burying seeds and nuts in the ground. They dig up these again in winter, when other food is hard to find. They can remember the exact location of hundreds of nuts, even when the ground is covered by snow. Many migrating birds also have good memories and return to the same nest site from thousands of kilometres away.

BIRDS THAT TALK

If you've been to a zoo, you have probably heard birds that can talk. Parrots are experts at imitating human speech. Budgies, which are small parrots, often learn many words. But talkative birds aren't quite as brainy as they seem. They don't understand what they are "saying". They are just copying sounds.

Stopping for a chat ▶
Budgies are best at learning words when they are young. They can even be taught to whistle tunes.

HANDY TIP

Try repeating the experiment a day later, to see if birds remember how to get at the food.

4 **See what happens** when the birds arrive and start to feed. To begin with, they will feed from the open pot. When that one is empty, see if any of them are brainy enough to open the lid of the other pot.

Starlings are some of the brainiest garden birds

All birds will eat from the open pot first

Flock watching

In the wild, many birds live in flocks. Some contain only a handful of birds, but the largest flocks can be more than a million strong. Birds flock together mainly for safety. In a flock, some birds can always be on the lookout, so it is harder for predators to take them by surprise. Flocking also helps birds to find scattered or patchy food. The flock searches like a team, so when one bird spots food, all the other birds join in.

Mobbing
In cities and in the countryside, look out for birds of prey being dive-bombed by smaller birds. This is called mobbing, and for small birds it is an important method of self-defence. By harassing the larger bird, they often manage to drive it away.

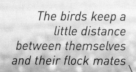

The birds keep a little distance between themselves and their flock mates

COUNTING UP

It is exciting when a big flock of birds flies overhead. But how can you work out how many birds there are? They always move too fast for you to count each one. Try dividing the flock into imaginary squares. Estimate the number of birds in a square and then multiply this number by the number of squares that fit over the flock. The result won't be exact, but is usually much closer than a guess.

◄ **Squares in the sky**
This flock has been divided into 16 imaginary squares. Some squares are full, but others are almost empty. The average number of birds per square is about five, making a 90-bird flock.

SENTRY DUTY

If you watch a flock feeding, you will see that they don't all eat at once. Instead, they take turns to keep their heads up so they can spot any sign of danger. If one bird spots trouble, it takes off and the rest of the flock instantly follows. This sentry system makes it harder for predators to attack.

All clear ▶
While its partners are busy feeding, one of these sparrows is looking up to check for danger. In large flocks, many birds need to be on sentry duty at any one time.

Mixed flocks
These gulls and knots have gathered together to forage for crabs or fish on a sheltered stretch of beach. At night, gulls usually roost on water. Knots and other shorebirds roost on beaches when the tide is high, and feed when it is low – during the day or the night.

Migration

If you get to know your local birds, you will notice that some are permanent residents – you can see them all through the year – and others are migrants. Migrants usually arrive in spring and stay throughout the summer, but when autumn begins, they disappear. Migrating birds often travel huge distances, but the effort is well worthwhile. They breed in the summer, when there is lots of food for their young. When they have raised a family, they fly to somewhere warm for the winter and return the following year.

Migrants on the move

Snow geese migrate up to 4,000 km (2,500 miles) between the Arctic and the southern USA. Like most migrating birds, they follow routes called flyways. Each flyway has "refuelling stops", where the geese take a break and feed.

FORMATION FLYING

Big birds, such as geese and cranes, often fly in V-formation when they migrate. This saves energy because each bird is helped by the swirling air from the one in front. The leading bird has to work hardest, so each bird takes a turn at the front. Birds migrate by day and by night. On clear nights in spring and autumn, look at the full moon through binoculars. You might be lucky enough to see migrating birds silhouetted as they fly past.

Long-distance travellers

In many parts of the world, spring is an exciting time for birdwatching because that's when most migrants arrive. Some migrants, including swallows, are easy to spot because they spend a lot of their time on the wing. Others stay well hidden. The best way to recognize these is by their calls.

Common cuckoo ▲

Throughout Europe and northern Asia, the cuckoo is a well-known migrant famous for its two-note call, which is impossible to miss.

Scarlet tanager ▶

This bird breeds in North America and winters in South America. Males are bright red in spring and summer, but they turn greenish-yellow once the breeding season is over.

GETTING READY TO GO

Departure lounge ▲
Before swallows migrate, they fly about restlessly, settling on roofs and wires and frequently preening their wings.

As summer draws towards an end, watch out for birds getting ready to migrate. Swallows often perch on telephone wires waiting for the big day when they set off. On the return journey, the males usually arrive first, often to the very same nesting site that they used the year before. Some migrants, including swallows, migrate in scattered groups, but many birds travel on their own. Amazingly, young birds find their way, even though they have never made the journey before. They are guided entirely by instinct.

▲ Ruby-throated hummingbird
This tireless migrant travels all the way from Central America to Canada, flying non-stop across the Gulf of Mexico.

Chiffchaff ▼
This common insect-eater arrives in northern Europe just as the trees are coming into leaf. Its "chiff chaff" call is a sure sign that spring is underway.

Swallow ▶
Swallows breed right across the northern hemisphere, arriving in mid-spring when the first insects are on the wing. North American swallows spend the winter in South America, while European ones head for Africa.

Bird calendar

If you're a keen birdwatcher, there is something to see all through the year. By keeping a bird calendar, you can record the highlights as the year goes by. If you have a camera, take some photos of the things you see and paste them on to the calendar. If not, try drawing some of the highlights yourself.

WHAT YOU WILL NEED

- A month-by-month calendar
- Pens and pencils • Glue
- Photographs of any birds you spot
- Feathers, pieces of eggshell, etc.

MAY

2

3 Woken by owls hooting this morning

4

7

8 Ducklings in park

9 Bird buffet **BIG SUCCESS**

1

14 Weather turning warmer

15 Saw sparrowha flying ove garden

20

21 Bird b insta

1 Find a calendar that has plenty of space for each day. Record what you see, adding pictures and things you have collected. For a long-term project, try comparing bird calendars from year to year to see how birds' behaviour is linked to the seasons.

KEEPING IN STEP

Spring

Birds don't know the time or the date, but they still keep in step with the seasons, and do the right things at the right time of year. In spring, the days get longer. Birds use this as a signal to migrate northwards, and to start making their nests.

Autumn

In the autumn, the days start getting shorter. This makes migrating birds head southwards. The change triggers other behaviour too. Many adult birds moult their feathers so they have a new set ready for the winter. Jays start storing food.

5 First cuckoo heard today

11 weather COLD AND WET!!

18 Nest box occupied!

6 First swifts seen today

17 Went to seaside – saw birds nesting on cliffs

24

22 Found some owl pellets

23 Feather collection started

30

Bird lifespans

Compared to humans, birds have very varied lifespans. Small songbirds often live for less than three years, while larger birds can survive well into their 40s. But before a bird can reach old age, it first has to get through the early months of its life. This is a dangerous time for birds. Many young birds are caught by predators, while others die from hunger or from cold. But because birds have large families, enough usually survive to raise young of their own.

Bird ringing
This young oystercatcher has been fitted with leg rings so birdwatchers can check its progress as it grows up. If you find a dead bird with a ring, look to see if it has an address on. Your find could provide useful information about survival in the wild.

The female calls softly to keep the ducklings in a group

Against the odds
If you watch ducklings during the spring and summer, you will see how tough life is for young birds. This female eider has lots of ducklings, but by the time summer arrives, she will probably have only two or three left.

BIRD BOOM

If all baby birds survived to become parents, birds would crowd out the skies. If you have a calculator handy, an easy sum will show you why. Starting with two adult blue tits, how many would there be after ten generations, if all their young survive? Blue tits lay about six eggs a year. To get the answer, just multiply six by itself ten times.

Fast families ▼
Blue tits have one family a year, but many songbirds have two or even three. They raise lots of young because only a few survive.

Ducklings' fluffy down helps to keep them warm

Success stories

Once a bird is fully grown, its chances of survival get much better. Compared to young birds, it is better at finding food and at keeping out of harm's way. How long it lasts will depend partly on luck, and partly on what kind of bird it is. Here are some examples of how long birds live in the wild.

Grey heron ▶
Herons can survive to be more than 20 in the wild, and even older in captivity.

Tawny owl ▶
For their size, owls are long lived birds. Tawny owls live to about 15. They start breeding at one year and, like most birds, keep breeding until they die.

House sparrow ▼
Compared to owls and herons, house sparrows have short lives. They rarely survive to be more than five, but have up to three families a year.

Helping birds

For many of the world's birds, life is not easy. Humans are changing the planet, and birds are finding it harder and harder to find the space and food that they need. There are about 10,000 kinds of birds on Earth, but already, one in eight of them is threatened with extinction. However, scientists and bird-lovers are working hard to help birds all over the world. If you like birds, you can join in too.

WHAT YOU CAN DO

- Look on the Internet or in your local telephone directory to find contact details for birdwatching organizations.
- Find out if there are any bird reserves near you and plan a visit.
- Make a trip to a zoo to see birds from all over the world.
- Tell your friends about birds and birdwatching. They can help as well.

Binoculars will help you to spot rare or unusual birds

Bird clubs
If you join a local birdwatching club, you can find out more about your local birds, and the problems that they face. Many birding clubs have links with much larger organizations, which work to protect birds all over the world.

INJURED BIRDS

Every year, many birds get injured by cars, by cats, or by getting tangled up in rubbish. If you find a badly injured bird, your chances of saving it are slim. However, if the bird is small, and you want to help, put it in a box lined with paper, with a beaker of water beside it. Leave the box somewhere dark and quiet indoors, then contact a bird club for help.

Grounded gull ▶
This young gull has got its leg trapped inside a plastic box. Gulls can peck hard, so you must handle a bird like this with caution. Ask an adult to help and contact a local animal rescue centre.

Bird zoos

The best place for any bird is in the wild, where it can fly free. But some zoos play an important part in bird conservation by breeding endangered species. Visiting a well-run zoo is a good way of seeing species from all over the world.

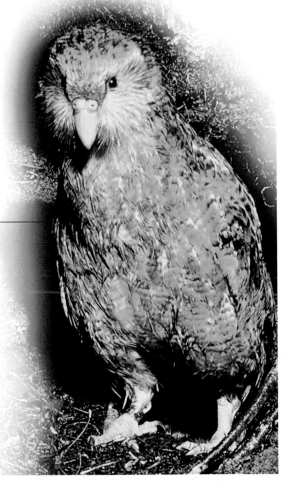

A kakapo's green plumage helps to camouflage it among grass and shrubs

Back from the brink

Some of the world's rarest birds are being helped by emergency action. In New Zealand, for example, wildlife experts are trying to save the kakapo, an extraordinary parrot that cannot fly. The kakapo is threatened by introduced predators, such as rats and cats. Without help, it would already have died out.

Bird classification There are about 10,000 different species of birds in the world. Scientists classify them into 30 different groups, called orders, based on key features that they share. The largest orders contain thousands of birds, while the smallest contain fewer than 10. On these two pages, you can find out about 12 of the most important orders of birds. Each order has two names. One is its scientific name. The other is its everyday name, which is the one normally used by birdwatchers.

BIRD	NAME OF GROUP	SPECIES TOTAL	KEY FEATURES	EXAMPLES
Heron	HERONS AND STORKS **Ciconiiformes**	119	Tall birds with long legs and long beaks. Herons and storks usually feed in or near water, but they roost in trees.	Grey heron White stork
Duck	DUCKS, GEESE, AND SWANS **Anseriformes**	149	Waterbirds with broad, flattened beaks and webbed feet. These birds are all good swimmers, but most are also fast and powerful fliers.	Mute swan Mallard
Eagle	BIRDS OF PREY **Falconiformes**	307	Predatory birds with hooked beaks, and powerful feet with sharp claws. Many birds of prey search for food by soaring high into the air.	Golden eagle Kestrel
Chicken	GAMEBIRDS **Galliformes**	281	Plump ground-dwelling birds with small heads and rounded wings. Instead of flying away from danger, they often run.	Chicken Common pheasant
Gull	SHOREBIRDS, GULLS, AND TERNS **Charadriiformes**	343	Birds that feed on the coast, or in damp places inland. Some of these birds dive for fish, but shorebirds search for food by the tideline.	Curlew Herring gull

BIRD	NAME OF GROUP	SPECIES TOTAL	KEY FEATURES	EXAMPLES
Pigeon	PIGEONS AND DOVES **Columbiformes**	309	Plump birds with small heads that bob backwards and forwards as they walk. Pigeons often feed on the ground, but are strong fliers with powerful wings.	City pigeon Diamond dove
Parrot	PARROTS **Psittaciformes**	353	Colourful and often noisy birds with hooked beaks and fleshy toes. Parrots are good climbers, and often feed in trees.	Cockatiel Rainbow lorikeet
Owl	OWLS **Strigiformes**	205	Predatory birds that hunt after dark, using keen eyesight and hearing. Owls have camouflaged plumage, which helps them to hide during the day.	Tawny owl Barn owl
Hummingbird	HUMMINGBIRDS AND SWIFTS **Apodiformes**	424	Superb fliers with stiff, slender wings. Hummingbirds feed on nectar by hovering in front of flowers. Swifts hunt insects in mid-air.	Ruby-throated hummingbird Common swift
Kingfisher	KINGFISHERS, BEE-EATERS, AND RELATIVES **Coraciiformes**	191	Birds with compact bodies and large beaks that often swoop on their food. Kingfishers dive into water, but bee-eaters feed in the air.	Common kingfisher European bee-eater
Woodpecker	WOODPECKERS AND RELATIVES **Piciformes**	380	Good climbers with strong toes that spend most of their lives in trees. Woodpeckers chisel into wood with their beaks to find food and to make nesting holes.	Great spotted woodpecker Yellow-bellied sapsucker
Thrush	SONGBIRDS **Passeriformes**	5,000+	A huge group of birds that often sing loud songs. Songbirds tend to be small in size.	Wren Blue tit Common cardinal House sparrow

Glossary

Albino A bird that has white areas in its plumage instead of the normal colour.

Bird of prey A bird that hunts other animals during daylight, catching them with its claws.

Bird pellet Indigestible food remains, which some birds cough up after they have had a meal.

Body feather A feather that gives a bird's body a smooth outline so that it can slip through the air. Body feathers are usually short and overlap like tiles on a roof.

Camouflage Colours or patterns that help a bird to hide, by making it blend in with its background.

Cormorant A bird that catches fish by diving underwater and kicking with its feet.

Courtship Behaviour that birds use to attract a mate so that they can breed. Courtship often involves special movements and displays.

Cuckoo A migratory bird that tricks other birds into raising its young. Female cuckoos lay their eggs in other birds' nests.

Dominant bird The leading bird in a group or a flock. The dominant bird often pecks the others to keep them in line.

Dove Doves are close relatives of pigeons. Some of them feed on fruit in trees, while others feed on seeds on the ground.

Down feather A fluffy feather that helps to keep a bird warm. Young birds often have thick down, particularly if they grow up in cold places.

Extinction When a species dies out completely. Many birds are threatened with extinction because humans are hunting them or taking over their habitats.

Fairy wren A long-tailed, seed-eating bird from Australia. Fairy wrens live in grassland and scrub.

Finch A small bird with a wedge-shaped beak that is specially shaped for cracking open seeds. Many finches live in large flocks.

Flight feather A feather from a bird's wings or tail. Flight feathers have a wide blade and a strong shaft, or quill.

Flightpath A bird's path through the air. Some birds have a straight flightpath, but others curve or bob up and down.

Flyway A route used by migrating birds. Flyways often follow features on the ground, such as mountain ranges and coasts.

Gannet A large seabird that catches fish by diving into the sea from high up in the air. Gannets' faces are specially protected against the impact of the dive.

Grebe A fish-eating bird that lives on freshwater and on coasts. Grebes' feet are set far back along their bodies, which makes them clumsy on land.

Habitat The kind of surroundings that an animal normally lives in. Bird habitats include grasslands, deserts, forests, coasts, and the open sea.

Honeyeater A medium-sized, nectar-feeding bird that spends most of its life in trees. Honeyeaters live in Australia, New Zealand, and on Pacific islands.

Hummingbird A small, nectar-eating bird that hovers in front of flowers to feed. Hummingbirds are found only in the Americas.

Jay A colourful member of the crow family that lives in woods and forests. Jays often bury nuts as winter food.

Kestrel A small bird of prey that spots its food by hovering high up in the air. Kestrels feed on small mammals and insects.

Kingfisher A colourful bird that swoops down on its food. Many kingfishers eat fish, but some catch animals on the ground.

Macaw The largest type of parrot. There are more than ten kinds of macaws. Many of them are in danger because they are caught and sold as pets.

Merganser A kind of duck that has a slender beak and lives underwater to catch fish.

Migrant Any bird that spends the winter in one place and the summer in another.

Migration Moving between summer and winter quarters.

Mobbing Ganging up on a larger bird to try to drive it away. Small birds often mob owls and birds of prey.

Moulting Shedding old feathers and replacing them with new ones. Most birds moult their feathers gradually once or twice a year.

Nesting colony A large group of birds nesting together.

Nightjar A night-flying bird that catches insects on the wing. Nightjars have large mouths, and they use them like scoops as they fly.

Ornithology The study of birds and the way that they live.

Owl A predatory bird that hunts at night. Unlike birds of prey, owls are very good at seeing in the dark, and they have keen hearing as well.

Parrot A colourful bird with a hooked beak. Most parrots live in warm places. They eat food from plants, including nectar, fruit, nuts, and seeds.

Pigeon A fast-flying bird that feeds on the ground and normally lives in a flock.

Preening Cleaning and rearranging feathers to keep them in good condition. Birds preen their feathers with their beaks and sometimes their feet.

Quill The shaft that runs down the middle of a feather.

Resident A bird that stays in the same area throughout the year.

Shrike A small bird with a hooked beak that catches lizards and other small animals.

Soaring A way of gliding high into the sky. A soaring bird spirals upwards inside columns of warm rising air.

Songbird A small bird that often sings to attract a mate. There are more than 5,000 kinds, including many garden and backyard birds.

Species A particular kind of bird. There are about 10,000 bird species – some are widespread, but others are found only in one place.

Starling A noisy, flock-forming bird with a sharp beak.

Swallow A migratory bird with a forked tail that feeds on insects in mid-air. Swallows often nest near houses.

Swift A migratory, insect-eating bird with crescent-shaped wings. Swifts catch their food in the air and sleep on the wing.

Tern A fish-eating bird with small legs and a sharp beak. Terns often flutter above the water before splashing down to catch their food.

Territory A piece of land that a male bird claims at the beginning of the breeding season. Males try to attract females into their territory to nest.

Thrush A ground-feeding bird that eats snails and worms. Many thrushes have attractive songs.

Tit A small, acrobatic bird that feeds in trees and bushes. Tits feed mainly on insects and often live in small flocks.

Webbing Skin between a waterbird's toes. When the bird kicks against the water, the webbing helps to push it along.

Woodpecker A bird that pecks holes in trees with its sharp beak. Woodpeckers live in woods all over the world, except Australia and New Zealand.

Wren A small insect-eating bird with a short, upright tail. Wrens often find their food by hopping over the ground.

Index

alarm calls 36
albino birds 32
avocets 50, 51
baby birds 45, 46–47, 65
baths 30–31
bats 55
beaks 4, 11, 19, 49
binoculars 6
bird callers 36–37
bird tables 14–15
birdfeeders 12–13
birds of prey 28, 58, 68
blackbirds 17, 32
breeding 34–35
budgies 57

calendars 62–63
calls 36–37
cardinals 35
chiffchaffs 61
classification 68–69
colonies 42
cormorants 24
courtship 34–35
crossbills 18
crows 19, 21, 47
cuckoos 60, 61
doves 29, 69
ducks 23, 35, 48–49, 64–65, 68

eggs 4, 44–45
equipment 6–7
eyes 5, 9
fairy wrens 35
feathers 4, 24–27
feeding 10–21, 48–49, 56–57
finches 29
flocks 58–59

flying 28–29, 55
footprints 22–23
gannets 43
gardens 16–17
geese 46, 48, 49, 60, 68
goldfinches 11, 16
grebes, great crested 34
guillemots 45
gulls 7, 23, 29, 32–33, 50, 52, 59, 67, 68

Harris's hawks 28–29
herons 22, 65, 68
hides 8–9
housemartins 43
hummingbirds 11, 13, 28, 61, 69
identifying birds 7, 32–33
jays 17, 19, 56

kestrels 44
killdeer 47
kingfishers 20, 53, 69
kittiwakes 42
lifespans 64–65
lorikeets 17
lyrebirds 37

macaws 26
magpies 27
mallards 49
markings 33
mergansers 49
migration 60–61
mimics 37, 57
moorhens 23
moulting 27
nestboxes 40–41

nests 38–43
nightjars 54, 55

ornithologists 5
owls 11, 21, 27, 45, 54–55, 65, 69
oystercatchers 50, 64
parrots 17, 25, 57, 67, 69
pellets 20–21
perching posts 20
pheasants 27
pigeons 23, 29, 55, 69
preening 25
robins 5, 14, 35, 44

seabirds 39, 42
seed dispensers 12–13
shelducks 49
shorebirds 50–51
shrikes 18
songbirds 23, 36–37, 64
sparrowhawks 44
sparrows 33, 39, 53, 59, 65
starlings 39, 53, 57
swallows 11, 43, 61
swans 48, 49, 68
swifts 29, 69
tanagers, scarlet 60
terns 35, 39, 50, 68
thrushes 18
tits 41, 45, 47, 65
town birds 52–53
turnstones 50, 51

waders 21
wings 4, 28–29
wood warblers 45
woodpeckers 19, 29, 41, 53, 69
wrens 11

Index Hilary Bird
The publisher would like to thank the following for their kind permission to reproduce their photographs:
(Key: a-above; b-below/bottom; c-centre; f-far; l-left; r-right; t-top)

4 Corbis: Ron Austing, Frank Lane Picture Agency (bl). **5 N.H.P.A.:** David Woodfall (tl); **Warren Photographic:** Kim Taylor (br). **6-7 Corbis:** Chris Rainier (c). **7 N.H.P.A.:** Roger Tidman (tr). **11 DK Images:** Kim Taylor (cra); **Warren Photographic:** Kim Taylor (tl). **13 Warren Photographic:** Kim Taylor (br). **15 Warren Photographic:** Kim Taylor (r). **17 Corbis:** Gary W. Carter (tl); **N.H.P.A.:** Daniel Zupanc (br); **N.H.P.A.:** Mike Lane (cr); **N.H.P.A.:** Rod Planck (cra). **18 FLPA:** images of nature: (tr); **FLPA:** - images of nature: S & D & K Maslowski (tr); **Nature Picture Library:** Dietmar Nill (c); **rspb-images.com:** Roger Wilmshurst (b). **19 FLPA:** images of nature: John Watkins (tl); **rspb-images. com:** George McCarthy (r); **Warren Photographic:** Kim Taylor (b). **20 Windrush Photos:** (bl). **21 Warren Photographic:** Kim Taylor (cra). **22 Warren Photographic:** Kim Taylor (br). **23 FLPA:** images of nature: David Hosking (tf). **24 Warren**

Photographic: Jane Burton (c); **Warren Photographic:** Kim Taylor (bl). **26-27 Corbis:** Farrell Grehan; **Warren Photographic:** Kim Taylor. **27 Ardea.com:** Piers Cavendish (cr). **28 Warren Photographic:** Kim Taylor (tc), (r). **31 rspb-images. com:** Bob Glover (t). **32-33 FLPA - images of nature:** Silvestris Fotoservice. **32 N.H.P.A.:** Mike Lane (b). **33 FLPA - images of nature:** Roger Wilmshurst (tr); **N.H.P.A.:** Nigel J Dennis (br). **34 N.H.P.A.:** Hellio & Van Ingen. **35 Alamy Images:** Gay Bumgarner (cra); **Ardea.com:** Pat Morris (tl); **Corbis:** Michael Gore; Frank Lane Picture Agency (br); **FLPA - images of nature:** Yossi Eshbol (bl); **N.H.P.A.:** Mike Lane (cr). **36. rspb-images.com:** Laurie Campbell (tr); **Warren Photographic:** (c). **37 N.H.P.A.:** Dave Watts (tr). **39. FLPA - images of nature:** Martin B Withers (br); **Windrush Photos:** (tr). **41 N.H.P.A.:** Andy Rouse (cr). **42 N.H.P.A.:** Laurie Campbell. **43 N.H.P.A.:** Stephen Dalton (t); **Still Pictures:** Jeremy Woodhouse (b). **44 Ardea. com:** M. Watson (c). **46 DK Images:** Guy Ryecart (c); **The Ivy Press Limited** (cr). **47 Corbis:** George McCarthy (b); **Corbis:** Lynda Richardson (tr). **48 FLPA - images of nature:** Michael Gore (bl). **49 FLPA - images of nature:** Steve Young (br); **N.H.P.A.:** Bill Coster (cla); **Warren Photographic:**

Kim Taylor (l). **50 Corbis:** George McCarthy (c). **51 Ardea.com:** B. Moose Peterson (b). **52 Alamy Images:** David Hoffman (bl); **N.H.P.A.:** Alan Williams (cla); **N.H.P.A.:** Manfred Danegger (cr). **54-55 N.H.P.A.:** Manfred Danegger. **55 DK Images:** Kim Taylor (b); **N.H.P.A.:** Mike Lane (c). **56 N.H.P.A.:** Alan Williams (bl). **57 Warren Photographic:** Kim Taylor (tr). **58-59 Corbis:** Kevin Schafer. **58 N.H.P.A.:** Nigel J Dennis (tr); **Warren Photographic:** Mark Taylor (bl). **59 DK Images:** Kim Taylor (t). **60-61 Alamy Images:** david tipling. **Corbis:** Chase Swift (cl); **Corbis:** William Manning (crb). **rspb-images.com:** Mark Hamblin (bc). **61 Corbis:** Annebicque Bernard (tr); **Corbis:** Joe McDonald (cbl); **Corbis:** Maurice Walker; Frank Lane Picture Agency (bcr); **rspb-images.com:** Gerald Downey (br). **63 Corbis:** Darrell Gulin (c); **Corbis:** Ralph A. Clevenger (ca). **64-65 Warren Photographic:** Mark Taylor. **64 Corbis:** Natalie Fobes (tl). **66-67 Alamy Images:** Joseph Sohm. **67 Alamy Images:** acestock (cl); **Crown Copyright: Department of Conservation Te Papa Atawhai:** (br); **RSPCA Photolibrary:** (tr). **78 Dorling Kindersley:** Greg and Yvonne Dean (ca). **79 Dreamstime.com:** Borislav Borisov / Filev (cla)
All other images © Dorling Kindersley
For further information see: **www.dkimages.com**

Blue-and-
yellow macaw

Crossbill

Mute swan

Pheasant

Robin

European
starling

Chukar
partridge

Goldcrest

Common
shelduck

Red-crested
cardinal

African
red-tailed
buzzard

Black-crowned
night heron

Crow

Kookaburra

Yellow-fronted
woodpecker

Nightingale

Bald eagle

Black
redstart

Eurasian jay

Lesser
flamingo

Blue tit

Eurasian
eagle owl

House sparrow

Magpie

Oystercatcher

Zebra dove

Song
thrush

Hoopoe

Rose-ringed
parakeet

Grouse

Nuthatch

Northern
oriole

Hawk

Dunnock

Kite

Coal tit

Grey wagtail

Blackbird

Pipit and
cuckoo chick

Pied avocet

Common
kingfisher

Jackdaw

Storks

European goldfinch

Great tit

Common swift

Scarlet macaw

Artic tern

Emperor goose

Curlew

Eurasian bullfinch

Skylark and chicks

Pigeon

Chaffinch